I am Kipper

Written by Roderick Hunt
Illustrated by Nick Schon,
based on the original characters
created by Roderick Hunt and Alex Brychta

OXFORD
UNIVERSITY PRESS

Read our names

I am Kipper.

I am Pam.

I am Mat.

I am Pat.

I am Tom.

I am Mac.

I am Sam.

Sam

Pat

Mat

Mac

Tom

Pam

Talk about the story

Missing letters

Choose the letter to make the word.

__op

__op

__ap

__op

Who did what?

Match each child with the right word.

tap

mop

hop

pop

The
Dog Tag

Written by Roderick Hunt
Illustrated by Nick Schon,
based on the original characters
created by Roderick Hunt and Alex Brychta

OXFORD
UNIVERSITY PRESS

Read these words

got	cat
top	cap
pot	mat
mop	tag

Kipper got a cat.

Biff got a top.

Chip got a cap.

Mum got a pot.

Dad got a mop.

Floppy got a mat.

Floppy got a tag.

Floppy sat on the mat . . .

. . . and he got a pat.

Talk about the story

Missing letters

Choose the letter to finish the word.

ca<u>t</u>

ca<u>p</u>

mo<u>p</u>

ta<u>g</u>

Rhyming pairs

Say the words. Find pairs of words that rhyme.

top

mat

cat

mop

A maze

Help Kipper to get to Floppy.